SUKI FERGUSON

THE SYMBOLIC TAROT

ARTWORK BY ANA NOVAES

THE SYMBOLIC TAROT
Mythic Meanings within Everyday Objects

Copyright © 2026 Suki Ferguson
Artwork Copyright © 2026 Ana Novaes

All rights reserved. Except for personal use, no part of this publication may be reproduced, in whole or in part, without written permission from the publisher. These cards are for spiritual and emotional guidance only and are not a substitute for medical advice or treatment. The author's views, within and beyond this publication, do not necessarily reflect those of the publisher. We respectfully request that this content not be used to train AI-generative models or machine learning systems without the publisher's written consent.

Published by Blue Angel Publishing®
10 Trafford Court, Wheelers Hill,
Victoria, Australia 3150
E-mail: info@blueangelonline.com
Website: www.blueangelonline.com

Edited by Cherise Asmah and Jules Sutherland

Blue Angel is a registered trademark of Blue Angel Gallery Pty Ltd.

ISBN: 978-1-922574-58-9

Printed on sustainably sourced paper,
with soy-based ink.

CONTENTS

INTRODUCTION 9
How to Use *The Symbolic Tarot* 13
How to Prepare a Question 15
Spreads to Try 16

THE MAJOR ARCANA 25
0. The Fool — Egg 26
1. The Magician — Hands 28
2. The High Priestess — Heart 30
3. The Empress — Rose 32
4. The Emperor — Jupiter 34
5. The Hierophant — Apple 36
6. The Lovers — Labyrinth 38
7. The Chariot — Horses 40
8. Justice — Swords 42
9. The Hermit — Oyster 44
10. The Wheel of Fortune — Coin 46
11. Strength — Jaguar 48
12. The Hanged One — Lotus 50
13. Death — Spent Blooms 52
14. Temperance — Weighing Scales 54
15. The Devil — Birdcages 56
16. The Tower — Fire 58

17. The Star 60
18. The Moon 62
19. The Sun 64
20. Judgement — Desert 66
21. The World — Eclipse 68

THE MINOR ARCANA 71

THE CUPS 73

Ace of Cups — Chalice 74
Two of Cups — Violet 76
Three of Cups — Bouquet 78
Four of Cups — Doorway 80
Five of Cups — Raven 82
Six of Cups — Child 84
Seven of Cups — Mushroom 86
Eight of Cups — Ladder 88
Nine of Cups — Vixen 90
Ten of Cups — Ribbon-bow 92
Page of Cups — Fish 94
Knight of Cups — Pearls 96
King of Cups — River 98
Queen of Cups — Humpback Whale 100

THE WANDS 103

Ace of Wands — Staff 104
Two of Wands — Bridge 106
Three of Wands — Mountain 108

Four of Wands — Garland 110
Five of Wands — Chains 112
Six of Wands — Chrysanthemums 114
Seven of Wands — Wolf 116
Eight of Wands — Fist 118
Nine of Wands — Deer 120
Ten of Wands — Burning House 122
Page of Wands — Salamander 124
Knight of Wands — Lioness 126
King of Wands — Keys 128
Queen of Wands — Sunflower 130

THE SWORDS 133

Ace of Swords — Sword 134
Two of Swords — Wall 136
Three of Swords — Storm 138
Four of Swords — Eyes 140
Five of Swords — Scissors 142
Six of Swords — Boat 144
Seven of Swords — Locked Box 146
Eight of Swords — Hurt Bird 148
Nine of Swords — Tears 150
Ten of Swords — Swan 152
Page of Swords — Window 154
Knight of Swords — Brain 156
King of Swords — Butterfly 158
Queen of Swords — Elder 160

THE PENTACLES 163

Ace of Pentacles — Hare-Coin 164
Two of Pentacles — Infinity 166
Three of Pentacles — Buffalo 168
Four of Pentacles — Cracked Mirror 170
Five of Pentacles — Yellow Carnation 172
Six of Pentacles — Cornucopia 174
Seven of Pentacles — Frog 176
Eight of Pentacles — Hammer 178
Nine of Pentacles — Rainbow 180
Ten of Pentacles — Contact 182
Page of Pentacles — Rabbit 184
Knight of Pentacles — Waterwheel 186
King of Pentacles — Peacock 188
Queen of Pentacles — She-Goat 190

About the Author 193
About the Artist 195

INTRODUCTION

THE SYMBOLIC TAROT IS A DREAMLIKE collaboration across languages, cultures, and continents, bridged by archetypes and associations. My name is Suki, and I'm a writer and tarot reader living in London, UK. Ana is an artist and illustrator living in São Paulo, Brazil. Our shared grammar for the co-creation of this deck has been a wide range of symbols that come within reach of being universal, polished by centuries of cross-cultural meaning-making.

Symbols are evocative beyond words. By placing symbolism at the heart of this deck, we hope to open up associative dreamscapes for you as a tarot reader. Ana provides the image, I provide the message, and you, the reader, provide the ever-shifting, catalytic third thing — the meaning.

Take the rose, which appears here in the Major Arcana, as *The Empress (3)*. The delicate scent of roses captivated the gardeners who first cultivated them in ancient China, and their beauty and evocative perfume are still celebrated around the world today. In every era, poets and singers have built the charms and dangers of roses into our psyches. Individuals can favour certain associations — roses may be fusty and outmoded to one person, while for someone else, they are charged with eros.

Then there are symbolic possibilities; a rose blooming in a desert suggests a miracle against deprivation; a trellised rose implies a leisured kind of order; and a rose in the tropics is a rarefied interloper, with many bright and luscious rivals. When a rose appears in the hand of a lover, a well-wisher, or someone in mourning, its essential rose-ness follows, even as its signification and presence tonally shifts in each context. And yet, your feeling about roses is a part of your interpretation of this card; and so you shape what *The Empress (3)* means.

Carl Jung, an early founder of analytical psychology and lover of all things esoteric, found his way to tarot through his exploration of archetypes and symbols. In his final book, *Man and His Symbols* (Doubleday, 1964), Jung wrote that, "What we call a symbol is a term, a name, or even a picture that may be familiar in daily life, yet that possesses specific connotations in addition to its conventional and obvious meaning." He added that a symbol implies something "vague, unknown, or hidden from us."

This vague, unknowable dream-quality is something that Ana has imbued in the imagery of this deck. There is softness and diffusion here, allowing edges to merge and blur. My accompanying text leaves space for questions, whilst offering an array of potential meanings for you to respond to.

An unspoken conversation between the artist, writer, and reader is sparked by every well-used tarot deck. In creating *The Symbolic Tarot*, we recognise and appreciate that wordlessness which sits alongside interpretations that are spoken or written.

We hope the symbols across cards tap into your associative instincts. For Jung, a true symbol contains an "unconscious aspect that is never precisely defined or fully explained. Nor can one hope to define or explain it. As the mind explores the symbol, it is led to ideas that lie beyond the grasp of reason." With this tarot, we encourage explorations of the gap between seeing and knowing.

REFERENCES

When we made this deck, we shared a reference book — the remarkable compendium of symbolic art and history, *The Book of Symbols: Reflections on Archetypal Images* (Taschen, 2010).

This multi-authored encyclopaedia of images and their biographies is dense with research and cultural variety — and it only skims the surface of its source, the Archive for Research in Archetypal Symbolism (ARAS). This archive holds a collection of over 18,000 images, selected for their rich symbolic meaning.

HOW TO USE *THE SYMBOLIC TAROT*

A simple way to get to know *The Symbolic Tarot* is to spend time with the cards in a quiet place, where you can spread out the deck freely and read this guidebook at your desired pace. Look at all the cards together, just to see which symbols are present.

When you shuffle this deck, you hold flowers, birds, keys, horses, an oyster, a frog, a jaguar, a heart, a planet, and much besides — alongside the classic wands, cups, swords, and coins. Below are some tips that will help you get to know them all better.

FOLLOW YOUR EYES
Which symbols attract your attention the most? Which feel mysterious to you? Move the cards around, assembling and mapping as you go, in whatever way pleases you — you can compare the four Aces, and then the four Pages, for example, or you could group all the cards that feature animals.

GIVE YOURSELF TIME
Get familiar with your cards by using them a little and often. It's fun to bring a new deck with

you out and about, so that you can pull a card whenever you like — when meeting a friend, on your lunch break before a busy afternoon, or whilst enjoying time in nature. Think of the deck as a companion to your usual life.

NOTICE LITTLE PROMPTS FROM YOUR ENVIRONMENT

Perhaps you see a bright star on a clear night; this is a moment for spending time with *The Star (17)*. Maybe you dream about the sea; look to the graceful humpback whale *Queen of Cups* for further inspiration. Or perhaps someone gives you sunflowers, which nudge you towards a different Queen, the sunflower-bearing *Queen of Wands*.

KEEP REVISITING THIS GUIDEBOOK

Once you've familiarised yourself with the cards as a whole, you'll be attuned to the presence of these powerful symbols around you. When prompted to think of a card, look up the description in this guidebook. You can carry only the booklet with you, if you prefer to keep the cards in a safe place at home.

DON'T WORRY IF YOU FORGET A CARD'S MEANING

Often, a card's message only becomes memorable when you need its particular guidance. In the meantime, enjoy the different moods and tones that arise as part of your deck-exploration.

HOW TO PREPARE A QUESTION

When preparing to read your cards, feel out a question that will direct the reading. First, think about your timeframe — is there an urgent situation you are seeking to explore? Focusing on a key date will clarify your reading, and make your outcome card relate closely to your dilemma. If you're looking at a more open-ended period of time—for example, if you are reading your cards for the year ahead—your reading may develop a new meaning that emerges as time passes.

An urgent, time-based question could look like: "How might I navigate the coming week?"

A more open-ended question could look like: "What is emerging for me?" This question would suit a spread that has upwards of five cards — inviting complexity. Or you can concentrate the question by pulling just one card, and observing how its themes appear over the coming week, month, or year.

SPREADS TO TRY

THE ONE-CARD PULL

Drawing one card at the start or close of each day is a time-honoured practice for getting to know a new tarot deck, as it enables you to focus on the full meaning of whichever symbol you happen to pull.

When you first draw a card, give yourself time to look at it closely. What do the colours feel like to you? What do you notice first? Do you feel recognition, or bafflement, or something else entirely? Let the card's imagery marinate for a minute before you look it up in the guidebook. Your very first encounter with a card may be memorable — card meanings tend to change over time as we change alongside them, so it can be interesting to recall your initial impression.

Once you've sat with the card's imagery for a while (when you close your eyes, can you visualise it?), look up the associated meaning. You'll find an entry that provides three keywords for the card, a description of the symbols and visual themes, and guidance on how to interpret the archetypal symbol in a reading. Finally, there is a reversed reading.

A THREE-CARD READING — THE 'RIGHT NOW' SPREAD
This reading takes very little time to do, whilst giving you a bracing look at your situation. Sometimes urgency is what's required! Try it when you want to have a quick and clarifying conversation with yourself.

Card One: What do I need to release, right now?
Card Two: What can I welcome in, right now?
Card Three: A direction I can choose, right now.

A FOUR-CARD READING — PAST–PRESENT–FUTURE–ADVICE

This reading is perfect for when you have a question to ask your cards that takes a general look at your situation, whilst offering a touch of counsel.

Card One: Past
Card Two: Present
Card Three: Future
Card Four: Advice

'Advice' can also be referred to as 'Outcome' or 'Your Next Step' — use a word that works for you. You can also shorten this reading to the classic three-card spread of Past–Present–Future. This simple spread is excellent for giving narrative shape to your current situation, whatever it may be.

A SEVEN-CARD READING — THE ELLIPSIS SPREAD

This seven-card spread is excellent for situations where you have a clear topic that you would like to address in some depth. The classic ten-card Celtic Cross Spread is ideal for holistic enquiries, for sifting through your life when things feel murky, and for grounding you when you feel unmoored. But sometimes you just need to get down to the nuts and bolts of a particular problem — and the Ellipsis Spread does this very well.

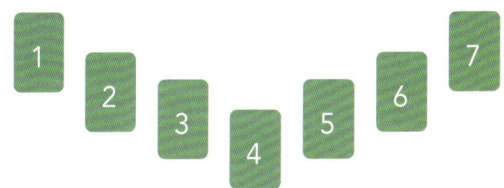

Card One: Past — pay attention to the aspect of your past that this card evokes.

Card Two: Present — how might this card relate to your present circumstances?

Card Three: Future — a possibility; do you embrace it, or want something different?

Card Four: Advice — seek out a positive course of action within this card's meaning.

Card Five: Outside Influence — a person or circumstance that commands your attention.

Card Six: Hope and Fear — does this card inspire you, or does it represent an outcome you dread? Take your response to the card as a nudge towards what you really want.

Card Seven: Outcome — consider the implications. You can work towards this outcome, or away from it.

A TEN-CARD READING — THE CELTIC CROSS
A classic tarot spread that provides a holistic view of your situation is the ten-card Celtic Cross. This widely used format is beloved by tarot readers for good reason — settling down to read a full Celtic Cross spread is a wonderful form of meditation and reflection.

Card One: The Heart of the Matter — your present situation.
Card Two: That Which Crosses It — a cross-current within your situation.
Card Three: Conscious Thought — something on your mind; a known factor.
Card Four: Root Cause — an unexplored factor; a key to the situation.

Card Five: Past — what has led to this moment.

Card Six: Future — an emerging mood; what is to come.

Card Seven: Your Role — a way of seeing yourself in this situation.

Card Eight: That Which Surrounds You — the setting or context in which this is happening.

Card Nine: Hopes and Fears — how you feel about the card that appears here decides whether it is a hope or a fear.

Card Ten: Outcome — a guidepost for your next steps.

THE MAJOR ARCANA

The Major Arcana is made up of 22 cards, numbered from 0 to 21. Each card of the Major Arcana relates to a universally significant life experience. These experiences are likely to emerge in your life somehow, and shape who you are as a person. Your innocent child-self is represented here as *The Fool (0)*, as are parental influences in *The Empress (3)* and *The Emperor (4)*. Your student self is here, and so is your teaching self, in *The Hierophant (5)*. *Death (13)* is here, and so is rebirth, in the form of *The Star (17)* and fulfilment — everything aligns in the last of these cards, *The World (21)*.

When cards from the Major Arcana appear in your readings, pay close attention. Sometimes, their significance feels daunting. At other times, their presence is a powerful affirmation of major shifts you know to be happening for you.

0. THE FOOL

- EGG • *Naivety – Risk – Wonder*

All life shares a miraculous state of flux: a bird's egg is alive, unconscious, and unborn; a butterfly is a caterpillar, gone. When roses bloom, they share pollen until their petals fall away. Each broken eggshell, empty chrysalis, and spent flower announces the innocent, unconscious courage of new life. Zero is the number of the Fool, a perpetual loop of nothing becoming something, and something becoming nothing.

IN A READING •

UPRIGHT: Have faith in the process. Birth, life, and death are ongoing. The present moment contains irresistible growth and renewal, alongside entropy. Vulnerability, loss, and breaking out of old forms are essential to becoming. Let these intertwined strands inspire you to seek out your next self. Follow your sense of wonder — it is a sure guide.

REVERSED: Something is amiss. You hoped for growth, but there is only a blight. Be patient. Over time, rot makes for rich compost.

1. THE MAGICIAN

- HANDS • *Power – Capacity – Skill*

Hands represent great possibility and high accomplishment. They can execute delicate tasks, provide the deftest of touches, shape music and art, meals and words. They can lift and carry and caress, or they can tear and punch and crush. Cultivation, tending, and undoing are all the work of hands.

Hands feel for us. They guide us when touch goes further than sight, and help us grapple with the unknown. And they tell stories without words; we see character in each other's hands, in differences of circumstance, and different attitudes of care. Hands signify what has been done, and what may be.

IN A READING •

UPRIGHT: You are capable of so much. Notice the presence of the four suits here: a pentacle, a sword, a cup, and a wand appear. *The Magician (1) is the only tarot card that holds every attribute — the powers of practicality, thought, emotion, and creativity. You are empowered to select the tool most fitting to your situation, and perhaps you will employ them in a bold combination. Think about your own abilities, and about all the things your hands have already learned and accomplished. Now is a good time to make preparations for a major endeavour, and to enjoy the resulting interplay of your talents.

REVERSED: Your abilities are not finding a suitable outlet and your ambition is becoming clouded by frustration. Try doing an activity completely unrelated to your dreams. Your spark will return.

2. THE HIGH PRIESTESS

• HEART • *Unconsciousness – Depth – Intuition*

The heart is central to survival, beating safely within its cage of bones, and it is linked to urges that resist reason: courage, love, grief, and care. *The High Priestess (2)* explores the power of subconscious instinct. The heart is pierced by a moon and a star, representing intuitions that arrive at night when logic is most quiet. And the heart rises above circles of white and black, bridged by a cross that symbolises divine union. Unlike the polarised colours, the heart is not simple, and it is not tidy. It is vital.

IN A READING •

UPRIGHT: There is truth in instinctive knowledge. Your mind can tell you a plausible story, but the beat of your heart is harder to gloss over. Your pulse reveals anxiety, excitement, contentment — it signals your animal state below the surface. The reasons for your reaction may be irrational or mysterious, but to ignore your heart entirely would be unwise. It beats solely for you.

What is your intuition saying? When you're unsure, listen to your heartbeat. Interpret its message. Are you driven by passion, alarm, or steady confidence? When you are able to tap into your heart's weather, you attain a bodily form of self-knowledge.

REVERSED: Shutting down your emotions is a survival strategy. If you feel numb in body and spirit, don't rush to feel again. Give your heart time to recover.

3. THE EMPRESS

• ROSE • *Sensuality – Presence – Love*

Fine scent, deep colour, soft petals, sharp thorns. Roses have been celebrated in poetry, art, and song for thousands of years. Between lovers, a single red rose is a romantic overture, and rose petals scattered on a bed signify luxurious eroticism. A colourful bouquet can be given to welcome a family's new baby, or celebrate a friend's accomplishment, or given as a peace offering from someone with some apologising to do. At a funeral, and on a grave, white roses signify grief. In every context, roses are a sign of intangible care made solid.

IN A READING •

UPRIGHT: *The Empress (3)* represents the nourishing and sensual aspects of physical femininity. A goddess visits you and presents you with a flower you can name with ease. She presses its stem into your palm even though its thorns prick at your skin. You breathe in the flower's fragrance. The goddess wants you to know that love is abundant, eternal, present in a million tiny moments, and that it blooms differently in each season of your life. Passion, care, affection, friendship, and romance are all bound up in this flower. Like a rose, love can be glorious, and wounding, and comfortingly familiar. *The Empress (3)* invites you to name and cherish the kind of love that matters most to you at this particular time.

REVERSED: Absence of loving care. Few people journey through life feeling continuously loved, or continuously loving. Moments of lovelessness connect you to the human experience.

4. THE EMPEROR

- JUPITER • *Order – Gravity – Responsibility*

Of all the planets in our solar system, Jupiter is the colossus. On clear nights, it is easily seen. Whirling storms travel endlessly across its surface, yet it is a reassuringly stable presence that has existed for billions of years. More than ninety moons orbit Jupiter; the sheer force of this gas giant's gravitational pull brings all kinds of space ephemera into orderly patterns.

A key provides control and protection to whoever holds it. Providing access—or removing it—creates the power of gatekeepers, guards, and kings. Exile and sanctuary are both implied. In Greco-Roman myth, the god of gods was Jupiter (or Zeus). He alone decided who would sit upon Mount Olympus, home of the immortals. *The Emperor (4)* is associated with conventionally masculine forms of power: of heft, protection, and setting the terms.

IN A READING •

UPRIGHT: There is something magnetic about a responsible person, and *The Emperor (4)* invites you to embrace this role. Chaotic forces may be at play around you, but your will is key: You can bring order.

Not every scenario will be resolved by consistency, logic, and power — but these attributes are often soothing. When you take care of business, you develop gravitas. Now is a good time to unlock the responsible part of yourself, and admire diligence in others.

REVERSED: Fixed rules and routines provide a feeling of safety, but they also cut you off from expansive experiences. An interruption to normal service can be a blessing in disguise.

5. THE HIEROPHANT

• APPLE • *Epiphany – Knowledge – Humility*

Reflexes aside, everything we do is learned. Humans are the slowest of all mammals to reach maturity, and we all depend on being taught. When circumstances are right, however, we can pick up knowledge very quickly. An apple teaches us how fast we move from ignorance to understanding, because a brief taste will reveal an apple's nature — a round, firm fruit may be sour, or sweet, or rotten at the core.

Apples are also catalysts. In the Bible and Quran, the original couple's taste of this forbidden fruit led to their banishment from Paradise. In Greek myth, the gift of an apple sparked discord that caused the Trojan War. The apple symbolises a simple yet loaded object, one that brings powerful aftershocks.

IN A READING •

UPRIGHT: The word 'hierophant' means teacher. The best teachers are eternal students — excited by discovery. Remember that change is constant, and that there is no one absolute truth, no one final way of knowing.

You can move from not knowing to knowing in an instant, and it can also take years of trying and failing. Learning involves accepting ignorance and failure. Practise acceptance, pay attention to your surroundings; greet all outcomes as valuable lessons. Firsthand experiences teach us well.

REVERSED: Learning can be obstructed by shame. Everyone learns at different speeds, and everyone experiences setbacks. We only fail when we lose hope in our ability to improve gradually.

6. THE LOVERS

- LABYRINTH   • *Devotion – Companionship – Reciprocity*

Holding the hand of a person you trust, you enter into the sacred geometry of a labyrinth. You and your trusted person have become partners. Together, you form intentions. You make decisions. You share responsibilities as they arise. Together, you encounter the inevitable dead ends. When this happens, you choose to stay with your partner, and your partner chooses to stay with you, too. Together, you wend your way towards the centre.

IN A READING •

UPRIGHT: "What does love require of us?", as the Quaker proverb goes. Real love requires that we enjoy companionship, and mutual care, and working things out as a team.

In a labyrinth, there is always a way through. Alone, you may face the puzzle as you like, choosing your pace and your path. With a partner, you adapt to their needs, and they adapt to yours. Disappointing setbacks and exhilarating successes are shared alike. *The Lovers (6)* is an invitation to appreciate interdependence as an integral part of love.

REVERSED: Romantically, you may feel stifled, or lovelorn, or that your happiness depends on having a significant other. Whatever the case may be, make time and space for doing things your way. You may as well enjoy being you, whether you're partnered or solo.

7. THE CHARIOT

- HORSES • *Will – Unity – Ambition*

Matched in strength, two horses represent oppositional powers. Progress is impossible when they are not aligned, and instead are using all of their strength to move in opposite directions. When they are united—harnessed to a chariot, for instance—their power becomes concentrated, and they are a force to be reckoned with. A journey that requires strength and speed can become light work when highly charged energies are combined using skill and purpose.

IN A READING

UPRIGHT: Recognise tension and alchemise it. To achieve a significant goal, your mind and your body need to work together. When you feel stuck, take a moment to identify any inner conflict that you are experiencing. Do whatever relaxes this inner conflict and allows you to move forward. Move your body, complete an errand, or meditate — and then tick off the next task of your important project. Experiment with what works for you.

As you begin to reconcile opposing tensions, your ability to focus on your goal will sharpen. And the more you focus the full force of your energy on your goal, the more progress you will make. *The Chariot* (7) celebrates your ambition to do great things, and your ability to overcome psychic obstacles along the way.

REVERSED: It's easy to give a lot of energy to a distraction. Switch to a horizon-scanning mode, instead of tunnelling ever deeper in the wrong direction. Check in with yourself and remember your ultimate goal.

8. JUSTICE

- SWORDS   • *Decisiveness – Righteousness – Mercy*

Two swords are perfectly straight. One, adorned by a mighty sun, points up to the heavens. The other points into the earth, its flame motif shadowed by a slender sickle moon. Upright, the sun-sword is primed for righteous and public action, fuelled by unrelenting fire. The downwards-pointing moon-sword signifies uncertainty. Its blade glows warmly, revealing the softening presence of mercy.

IN A READING •

UPRIGHT: Justice is a public expression of love, care, and protection, of taking all things into consideration, and providing a balanced response. The presence of two swords here emphasises the need for multiple tools and multiple points of view. The sun and the moon are different entities, each rich in meaning. One represents light and insistent knowledge; the other represents shade and fluctuating awareness.

The presence of *Justice (8)* in your reading invites you to view the feeling of anger positively. Raise your sun-sword against transgressions, and fight without apology for what is right. Temper this blazing energy with circumspection; employ the introspective, doubting moon-sword when a cooler mode of problem-solving is needed.

REVERSED: You feel paralysed when witnessing injustices beyond your control, whether these are brutalities of global conflict or cruelties closer to home. You do not have to be a bystander: Live your values by taking unambiguous actions within your sphere of influence.

9. THE HERMIT

- **OYSTER** • *Solitude – Alchemy – Self-Expression*

A pearl begins as a speck of grit, a grain of sand, a foreign body. Only the inner workings of the oyster can transform that intrusion into something so lustrous and singular; a gleaming nacre orb that catches the light as soon as it leaves the dark.

A solitary oyster protects its soft parts with a rough shell, and could be mistaken for any old rock as it performs its unwitnessed internal magic.

IN A READING

UPRIGHT: *The Hermit (9)* invites you to develop and choose your own forms of play, practice, ritual, and rest. Start by banishing the need to perform for others. Seek privacy and luxuriate in your solitude: Things may become more enjoyable when no one is making demands on you. Please yourself and appreciate your idiosyncrasies.

If the idea of spending time alone feels desolate or unsatisfactory, pay attention to your inner world. Self-expression can help you make a pearl from any grit embedded in your spirit. Time allows new layers to accrue and grow strong. Create whatever it is that you want, and make it shine.

REVERSED: Blocking out the world entirely can lead to atrophy — mental, physical, and spiritual. Go out, try new things, and observe different ways of being.

10. THE WHEEL OF FORTUNE

- COIN • *Luck – Fate – Character*

The square at the centre of this coin enables the bearer to string many such coins together. In Imperial China, such coins were currency, flowing between people. Then new coins were made, and the circle-square coins became worthless — until they came to be prized as good-luck charms. Though historic forces altered their fate, these coins are still valued, and still circulated. The ouroboros that encircles this coin is a mythic serpent that eternally devours its own tail. It destroys itself and feeds itself in one motion, and is complete.

IN A READING

UPRIGHT: What is a revolution? A full rotation, right back to the beginning. The coin may spin, and the serpent may look down or look up, but the essence remains intact. You can respond to luck the same way. No one type of luck lasts forever, and we are each subject to twists of fate. You'll experience good luck and bad luck — your spirit is the constant. Let yourself be known by how you respond to whatever fate throws your way.

REVERSED: *The Wheel of Fortune (10)* reversed suggests that you are protecting yourself from risk, and missing chances as a result.

11. STRENGTH

- JAGUAR • *Resilience – Self-Acceptance – Serenity*

A jaguar exudes sheer power. These apex predators do not rush: they prowl, they lounge. Their strength is attractive and unforgettable, intrinsic to their presence, and entirely natural. This jaguar makes no particular effort to be what she is.

Jaguars are independent by nature, able to provide for themselves and live life at their preferred pace. They are also shy without being timid, solitary without being lonely, strong without being argumentative. They exude a kind of calm forcefield that invites respect.

IN A READING •

UPRIGHT: Think about positive traits that you embody without effort. Perhaps you are naturally compassionate, or funny, or athletic. You are distinct; you have character. Meditate upon your strengths. This card says that you bring a particular energy into the world, and that it is valuable. If you tend to downplay your qualities, resist that urge. Act from the best part of yourself without apology.

REVERSED: Using a persona is smart in certain contexts, but continually masking your true self is soul-sapping. Be authentic when and where you feel able to do so.

12. THE HANGED ONE

• LOTUS   • *Stasis – Patience – Acceptance*

A lotus flower is suspended in the darkness, unmoored from the water, mud, and sunlight that once gave it context. In order to bloom, the lotus grows from darkness towards light. Outside of the logic of this ecosystem, it hovers and we see stasis: not growing, not dying. It continues to exist in the pause. Is this a peaceful break from the rigmarole of living, or is it an unwanted arrest? Either way, this upended lotus remains open and present.

IN A READING •

UPRIGHT: *The Hanged One (12)* invites you to breathe deeply. If you've been in action mode lately, it is time to take a break. If you are feeling stuck and stagnant, it is time to accept this moment and see what you may learn from it. Strange comfort can be found in being busy, pressured, and stressed out, particularly within value systems that prize productivity, convenience, and money above all. *The Hanged*

One (12) subverts the imperative of 'busyness'. Release yourself into stillness. Suspend activity. Lean into the discomfort. Meditate, and appreciate the evolution of your thoughts.

REVERSED: A period of letting things be and lying fallow is coming to an end. Enjoy renewing your efforts — connect with whatever brings you energy, or makes a useful demand on your time.

13. DEATH

- SPENT BLOOMS
- *Endings – Renewal – Inevitability*

A flower has bloomed, and an eclipse blocks the light. Night falls, and the petals will drop away and become part of the earth. The time for growth and fullness has passed, and the next phase begins. The Sun starts to return, slow and sure.

There is poetry in loving the sweet promise of a flower, and relating to its budding, blooming, and decay. But really we are the plant itself, rooted deep in the earth. A period of cold and quiet and loss can be weathered.

IN A READING •

UPRIGHT: Change is the only true constant. It can't be argued with or wished away. It's better to live with it, as we do the turning tides, and the rising and setting of the Sun.

When you see *Death (13)* in a reading, ask yourself what is coming to a natural end. Acknowledge it, and give yourself time to adjust. Renewal is coming — what might that be like?

REVERSED: Something that you hoped would end is continuing. Make peace with this for now, and look out for signs of change.

14. TEMPERANCE

- WEIGHING SCALES • *Balance – Nourishment – Equilibrium*

These equally weighted scales stand half on land, half in water. A star shines above the scales' fulcrum. Water spills from the weighing dishes, replenishing both the pool and the soil below. In the distance, mountain slopes can be seen. These are symbolic of a spiritual balancing act — to climb closer to the heavens, you grapple with the earth. We can experience depletion, strength, and enrichment, all in one go.

IN A READING •

UPRIGHT: Take a step back and survey aspects of your life: friendship, family, work, spiritual practice, community, love, sex, health, finances, and more. When thinking in this holistic way, you can see where they blend and sustain each other. You may also see aspects that have been sacrificed in favour of prioritising others; now may be a good time to nourish these a little more. *Temperance (14)* counsels you to aim for a free-flowing evenness over perfect, unchanging fullness. Strive, rest, and refuel; strive, rest, and refuel.

REVERSED: One aspect of your life is making special demands on you and, for the time being, that can't be ignored. Balance is a dynamic process — things will even out again in due course.

15. THE DEVIL

- BIRDCAGES
- *Craving – Temptation – Dependence*

Two heavy iron cages create a trap, where the bait is whatever you want it to be — something that appeals to your most destructive need. The five-pointed pentagram points downwards, a symbol of being pinioned by earthly desires, unable to ascend or escape. Cages represent the end of freedom, a drastic curtailment of agency. Cages also tempt us with the cold comfort of helplessness, which can be seen when we resign ourselves to familiarity instead of opting for change.

IN A READING

UPRIGHT: *The Devil (15)* can represent either a tyrannical external force in your life—someone who has power over you—or your inner trickster, who must be indulged. In either case, *The Devil (15)* refers to demands that must be obeyed, no matter what the cost may be to yourself and to others. Need is hard to bargain with. It can take many forms — *I need a drink; I need this win, that relationship; I need this job, this money, those clothes, that house.* Most needs make perfect sense. At the same time, it's easy to become so preoccupied with them that you hurt yourself and others in the process.

When you see *The Devil (15)*, beware of assigning undue power to external pressures. Set boundaries for yourself and honour them. Revel in your own free will.

REVERSED: You have everything you thought you needed, and yet you feel dissatisfied. To offset this feeling, think about aspects of your life that inspire a feeling of gratitude in you.

16. THE TOWER

- FIRE • *Rupture – Chaos – Aftermath*

Fire burns away whatever has gone before. To make fire, some solid thing must go up in smoke, whether it be the wick and wax of a candle or the trunk of a tree that has grown for a thousand years. Fire is no respecter of age or status — it is egalitarian in its chaos.

Though fire can humble us with its unpredictable, ravenous nature, it also has generative powers: After a wildfire, new growth emerges from the ashes.

IN A READING

UPRIGHT: *The Tower (16)* counsels you in moments of grievous disruption. Whatever you relied upon, and felt sure of, is suddenly gone. Shock and unreality follow. How is it that we can't prepare ourselves for such twists of fate or acts of God?

Try to accept the searing nature of total change. Survive it, and grieve what has been lost. Sensitivity follows suffering — give yourself time to recover. An unfamiliar future will gradually begin to take shape, and you will find that unexpected happiness awaits you.

REVERSED: It's natural to spiral a little after a shock, even if the shock is relatively minor. Breathe deeply, take care of your immediate needs, and sift facts from fears. Wait for calm before making big decisions.

17. THE STAR

- *Faith – Hope – Soul-Care*

A vast star burns white-hot over the ocean. Its pure form of energy fills the night sky — a glowing, sparking, natural radiance that refuses to be limited or extinguished. No artificial light competes with this star. It is complete and as close to eternal as we can conceive; it will burn and burn and burn, no matter what goes on here on Earth.

IN A READING

UPRIGHT: You are entering a gentle time of renewal and replenishment. This isn't easily come by — you've lost hope at times, and wondered if things would ever feel right again. When *The Star (17)* appears in your reading, however, blessings accompany it. A star is an unassailable point of light in the darkness.

This card recognises that having faith in the goodness of life can be difficult. Plenty of terrible things can outnumber what is good. Remember that a star is not always visible, and yet it still continues. Give loving care to your soulful self, the part of you that feels the magic of being alive.

REVERSED: The routines of day-to-day life have you feeling placid yet numb. The dark/light, hope/despair contrasts of *The Star (17)* feel alien. How have you dispelled this clouded feeling in the past? What is it protecting you from, today?

18. THE MOON

- *Mystery – Illusion – Divergence*

Darkness and the Moon playfully reveal and conceal ordinary things. A sunny landscape seems transformed at night — made strange by shadows and moonbeams. The Moon embodies unconscious power, pulling invisibly at tides of water and of blood. Moon cycles create an illusory sense of inconstancy, whilst remaining broadly dependable. The Moon is a friend to witches, werewolves, and shamans — and those who revel in familiar strangeness.

IN A READING

UPRIGHT: Mystery is a beautiful, vaporous thing, and when daylit logic comes calling, mystery disappears. Irrational whims and weird fantasies are the special domain of *The Moon (18)*. This card invites you to unlock your lunar self, the feral part of you that could howl and scream and run naked in the moonlight. Maybe doing so is wise — or maybe not. We all wax and wane in our madnesses. When this card appears, ask yourself: "What is my relationship to the darker, wilder aspects of myself, and of life in general?"

REVERSED: Giving your wildest dreams free rein involves risk. Fantasies may begin to block out reality; visualising what you want may disguise what actually is. Revisit the practical aspects of your situation.

19. THE SUN

- *Appreciation – Vitality – Confidence*

The Sun makes everything possible; it creates living proliferation, and sears it away. The Sun is both unthinkably distant and our most familiar friend. It has burned for over four billion years, and will burn for billions more, its unceasing combustion throwing heat and light into our universe. The Sun is the most eternal material thing that any person can witness, and though we are all touched by its power, we will never truly know it. Instead, we can accept its blessings: everything that lives.

IN A READING •

UPRIGHT: *The Sun (19)* is here to affirm your whole being. Appreciate yourself, as you might appreciate the Sun for rising. Notice your own inner fire. Think of your particular blessings; allow yourself to feel the happiness they bring you, and be radiant.

If you knew that everything would turn out okay, what would you do? Bring the alchemy of warmth and confidence to this endeavour. See it flourish, slowly and surely.

REVERSED: Your most recent setback has knocked your self-esteem. Remember that everyone—even the sunniest person you know—has bad days. Like the Sun itself, you are still here, still vital, still you.

20. JUDGEMENT

- DESERT • *Undoing – Accountability – Calling*

The desert is an inhospitable place, and here a stand of trees has been dried to kindlewood by the burning sun. In allegory, the desert is where spiritual wanderers are tested. A person who laments their misfortune and lacks faith may quickly give up. A person who seeks to understand their circumstances, and believes in their ability to survive, may well emerge from the desert transformed.

IN A READING •

UPRIGHT: *Judgement (20)* calls upon you to be real with yourself, to look at your life in the light. Judgement, in the Bible, refers to being called to a higher plane; ascending towards divinity. This card refers to searching for—and finding—a vocation. Focus on your calling. Your path may be difficult, but you won't feel lost.

In more general usage, the word 'judgement' can bring up feelings of shame or guilt. Give grace to these very human emotions; they can show you where to go next. Move away from shame and guilt by acting in alignment with *your* values. Let them motivate you to step towards your higher purpose.

REVERSED: While others feel motivated, you feel nothing much. Some rest and time alone may be beneficial. Questing requires energy; give yourself what you need before setting yourself a new challenge.

21. THE WORLD

- ECLIPSE • *Completion – Alignment – Interdependence*

For millennia, stargazers have harnessed the power of anticipation, movement, and fulfilment. Those who worshipped the Sun, Moon, and stars mapped out phenomena that could be predicted: solstices, meteor showers, orbits, and eclipses. Years of following the paths of celestial bodies meant that people could prepare for auspicious days, and share in great feasts and rituals together. When everything aligns, everybody rises to the occasion.

IN A READING

UPRIGHT: A moment of pure alignment with the universe. The presence of *The World (21)* in your reading heralds the culmination of a much-longed-for outcome. When careful effort is met with cosmic luck, miracles happen. These transitory experiences are to be hoped for, enjoyed, and treasured.

Notice where your relationships with other people bring special meaning to your endeavours. Remember that you belong in the world, and that you are part of something vast, complex, and complete.

REVERSED: Different elements of your life are in tension, and you feel stuck. Prioritise the element that takes you where you want to go. Give the rest time to align — eclipses are rare events.

THE MINOR ARCANA

Of the 78 cards in this deck, 56 belong to the Minor Arcana. Evolving from playing cards, the Minor Arcana is divided equally into four distinct suits, with each suit focusing on a core aspect of human experience.

Cards in the Minor Arcana echo many of the themes found in the Major Arcana, but they invite a slightly more day-to-day feeling than their Major cousins. So the *Five of Cups* suggests loss and grief, but in a softer way than either *Death (13)* or *The Tower (16)*. Several cards—the *Eight of Cups, Four of Swords* and *Six of Swords*—refer to various forms of retreat, but *The Hermit (9)* will convey this message loudest.

The four suits of the Minor Arcana are the Cups, the Wands, the Swords, and the Pentacles. Each suit contains 14 cards. They are numbered from Ace to Ten, and then there are four court cards — the Page, the Knight, the King, and the Queen.

THE CUPS

In tarot, Cups are vessels for containing water, and water symbolises emotion, spirituality, and intuition. The Cups is the suit that appreciates your soulful qualities, and addresses the ebb and flow of your emotional life.

Water is highly symbolic throughout *The Symbolic Tarot* and through tarot in general; notice how it appears in the form of droplets, vapour, clouds, rivers, tears, and seas.

Wherever a cup lies on its side, painful feelings such as loss and grief are being recognised.

Wherever water is cupped in these cards, emotions are being felt and respected. Your emotions are precious, and variable, and infinite, and the cup holds them tenderly.

ACE OF CUPS

- CHALICE • *Love – Trust – Soulfulness*

At the beginning of the Cups suit, a shining Ace welcomes you. This silver chalice is adorned with a delicate vine motif that bears fruit in all seasons, whether the cup is full or empty. The fine filigree denotes how precious the contents of the chalice may be. Lightness and gravity are both present: the cup floats above a cloud while a planet orbits it. The turquoise waters below are tranquil. A soft, spacious quiet suffuses the scene.

IN A READING •

UPRIGHT: Love is present. Think of it like water — it takes many forms. Water becomes cloud, cloud becomes rain, rain replenishes the earth. Each form matters. Take this cup as a vessel for love, and hold it out to the universe. Trust that it will be filled, and when it is, drink. Express the love you feel, too — chalices are meant for sharing.
Real love is wholesome. You may not always be loved in the exact way you expect to be, so be

sure to notice when love appears in unfamiliar gestures, fleeting moments, and everyday interactions.

REVERSED: If you find yourself doubting your ability to love, listen to your most soulful and optimistic self. Love that part of you, and protect it from cynicism. Trust the love you feel for small things.

TWO OF CUPS

- VIOLET   • *Opposition – Equality – Exchange*

The colour violet is created by the equal presence of two strong primary colours: red and blue. When these colours are blended with care, they create a shade that possesses its own beauty and vibrance. In this card, a rich fall of violet fabric envelopes this person, cloaking them with warmth, comfort, and grace as they move towards the unknown.

IN A READING •

UPRIGHT: The *Two of Cups* subverts the tensions of difference. You're well-matched in a partnership when you both experience the flow of togetherness and the clash of opposition. What begins as a swirl of mixed-up elements can be blended into something bespoke. When you are both open to flex and change in your relationship, a beautiful new 'colour' will emerge between you, one that's uniquely yours.

REVERSED: An intriguing relationship that resists definition. You enjoy the thrill of novelty and mystery that this new person brings you. If it starts to feel shadowy, it may be time for a primary colour.

THREE OF CUPS

- BOUQUET • *Friendship – Harmony – Joy*

Making a bouquet involves harmonising the particular beauty of different flowers. Each bloom enhances the distinctive qualities of its closest companion — one flower might be crisply scented and sinuously stemmed, while its neighbour can be leafy and bright. A bouquet's overall character is made through variety, contrast, and balance; colours become more vivid, the perfume more nuanced.

IN A READING •

UPRIGHT: Complementary differences create a magic that sameness cannot match. The *Three of Cups* celebrates togetherness, and the way that we can be fully ourselves around our chosen family. Notice how the creamy yellows contrast well with the shades of lilac. When you are with your closest friends, you draw out each other's idiosyncrasies, and enjoy them. You are each spectacular alone; when you are together, you are a whole other kind of spectacular.

REVERSED: Group dynamics can trigger insecurities. Tensions rise when you or others feel threatened. Remember, it's okay to be human and make mistakes — self-acceptance is relaxing. Seek out what you appreciate in yourself and in other group members.

FOUR OF CUPS

- DOORWAY • *Opening – Refusal – Capacity*

Three cups stand together in the foreground, their upright position referring to the presence of positive emotions. A fourth cup emerges between the half-open doors. Or are they half-closing? This imposing doorway can be flung open, or firmly shut. Which side would you prefer for this new cup to be on?

IN A READING •

UPRIGHT: The prospect of a new experience can be delightful — at the right moment in time. At the wrong moment, it can be overwhelming and unwelcome. The fourth cup in this card relates to a new emotion, and likely a positive one. Consider what might prompt this — a new role, a new friendship, a new project, or a new relationship. If you feel bored with your lot, and that life is passing you by, it's time to open the doors wide.

REVERSED: Given your current occupations, would adding something new create further stress, or cause you to neglect what you already have? If so, consider shutting the door. Listen to the feeling that follows — is it relief, or regret?

FIVE OF CUPS

• RAVEN • *Loss – Grief – Healing*

A raven—a representative of death, memory, and transformation—gazes at two cups. One of them teeters, at risk of falling, and the other lies on its side. The fallen cup represents a loss. The leaning cup represents the possibility of another. The raven is transfixed by these cups, and doesn't see the three that remain upright. A little bridge in the distance speaks of journeying from one place to another — from the grief of the present, to a future where unknown contentment becomes possible again.

IN A READING •

UPRIGHT: Grieve with a full heart. Loss tends to be re-experienced over and over, on waking and in unexpected everyday moments. Remembering your loss will be both an intrusion and an honour. Accept grief's presence. Cherish people who remain good and steady and available to you despite your distress.

As you heal, create new routines and follow your desires. Gradually, the present will matter to you again, and you'll find that your experience of mourning is a bridge that connects you to others.

REVERSED: After loss, escaping from what's left or drowning your sorrows has a certain logic. But in muting painful memories, what else is destroyed?

SIX OF CUPS

- CHILD • *Innocence – Nostalgia – Wonder*

A child experiences the world for the first time, wide-eyed and susceptible. And every emotion a child experiences may be gigantic, amazing, terrifying — a fully physical event, accompanied by tears, screams, or giggles. This mind-blowing state of being is ephemeral. It doesn't take long for children to learn to respond to new experiences with smaller reactions.

IN A READING

UPRIGHT: Memories that stay with you for life are ones infused with potent emotion. Some memories are dramatic, and some are gentle. Remembering can have the curious effect of softening what was once intense.

Generate the spark of sheer wonder by leaning into new experiences with childlike appreciation. Your inner child is always within you.

REVERSED: Reminiscing about good times gone by can block you from existing in the here-and-now. Enjoy the advantages of your current situation.

SEVEN OF CUPS

- MUSHROOM • *Imagination – Fantasy – Inaction*

Magic exists in us. Phantasms and daydreams emerge from the tender, commonplace material within our skulls. The veil between reality and imagination becomes thin at times, whether or not we want it to. Some visions can disturb us, while others can connect us, as a mushroom's spores reinforce the delicate strands of mycelium that underpin whole ecosystems.

IN A READING •

UPRIGHT: You carry multiple visions within you — hopes for the future, memories of the past, hallucinations conjured in fevers, revels, or rituals. You're capable of making any visions more solid, especially through sharing them with others. Scatter these microscopic particles of magic far and wide, and they will take root within a wider network.

REVERSED: Don't resist decay. Mushrooms thrive on rot, existing in the liminal space between life and death. If a dream dies, trust that a new one is emerging.

EIGHT OF CUPS

• LADDER • *Retreat – Withdrawal – Intention*

Each rung of a ladder takes its climber up and away from the steady ground. Usually, there is a specific endpoint, and a task to be accomplished there. Here, the ladder's purpose is undefined — there is simply a need to move away from the cups below, which are all filling up. The height of a ladder grants whoever climbs it a new vantage point, one that they bring with them back to earth.

IN A READING •

UPRIGHT: The *Eight of Cups* is a card that invites you to put a little bit of space between you and any emotional intensity — even the good feelings! Solitude is part of this card's message: This ladder is just for you. And climbing a ladder involves being intentional about your perspective; it's a brief holiday from your familiar view. Get your head above the clouds to see things afresh.

REVERSED: Ladders aren't really made for lingering on — if time out is leaving you at a loose end, return to your usual grounding routines.

NINE OF CUPS

• VIXEN • *Contentment – Fullness – Ease*

Foxes are tricksters, wily and prowling, born to survive by their wits. Mostly nocturnal, they are associated with shadows and stealth. Yet this fox sits proudly on a rock, unworried about being seen. Her relaxed pose speaks of her contented mood, and nothing threatens her equanimity. She is simply minding her business, enjoying being a fox, and happy in her own skin.

IN A READING

UPRIGHT: Imagine eating so much delicious food that you doze off, entirely content. The vixen of the *Nine of Cups* wants this feeling for you. Notice places where you feel safe, secure, and happy, and spend time in them. Indulge in whatever you enjoy, without apology. Do whatever makes you feel cheerful and relaxed. This could be as simple as sitting in a patch of sunlight, just because it feels good.

REVERSED: Responsibilities prevent you from feeling leisurely. Lean into the demands, but include your needs among them. Arrange a little date for yourself — just you, doing what *you* like.

TEN OF CUPS

- RIBBON-BOW
- *Happiness – Togetherness – Fun*

A pink silk ribbon tied in a bow is a delicate form of knot. Its presence suggests peace and pleasure. Delightfully impractical, a silk bow adorns and ties together things that are easily held. There is loving intention in its crisscrossing of fabric. Beauty and softness can be seen in the bonds that we choose to fashion for ourselves.

IN A READING

UPRIGHT: The *Ten of Cups* brings precious kinds of happiness right into your reading — sweetness and silliness, which can only really be enjoyed when we feel safe and secure. Revel in your lightest bonds. Seek out whoever it feels most fun to be with. Play games, dance, laugh until your cheeks hurt! Everyone deserves to have fun. Give yourself frivolity, just because!

REVERSED: Consider the aggravation of being told to "turn that frown upside-down!" Dysfunction is often covered up with forced fun — be cautious of those who insist on manufacturing the appearance of joy.

PAGE OF CUPS

- FISH • *Exploration – Curiosity – Openness*

For fish, water is their element, and in tarot, water represents emotions. Here, two fish symbolise all who swim with confidence in emotional currents. A fish has no sense of past or future; it lives sleekly in the present. Certain depths and rapids may suit these fish best, but they have the capacity to explore, too. From still shallows and strong rapids, wherever a river flows is within their reach.

IN A READING •

UPRIGHT: You are becoming more and more comfortable with experiencing the full range of your emotions. The presence of the *Page of Cups* suggests that being open to new connections and experiences is an emerging part of your emotional education. Embrace new possibilities, live in the now, and go with the flow. An easygoing resilience can come from treating each emotion as a teacher and friend.

REVERSED: Encouragement in pushing your boundaries can be invigorating, but you are approaching your limit. Listen to your inner voice.

KNIGHT OF CUPS

- PEARLS • *Perception – Contrast – Favour*

Two pearls gleam in the moonlight. Their contours are irregular, reflecting light and bringing lustre to their surroundings. There is a black pearl, and a white one. Each is entirely natural, and as it is meant to be. They may well be perceived differently, appreciated differently; they are equals in substance, yet fashion and favour may dictate their respective value.

IN A READING •

UPRIGHT: Note the duality of these pearls, alongside their basic sameness. This *Knight of Cups* may refer to a person who provokes powerful feelings, whether that's aversion or attraction. They may be a person of rare beauty, poetry, and soulfulness; they may also be prone to inconsistency or impracticality. There is brightness, shadow, and grit within the pearl. This person may be prized or devalued; remember that treasure is in the eye of the beholder.

REVERSED: You want someone to change, and their failure to do so frustrates you. This blocks you from seeing them as they really are. Go beyond accepting their 'flaws' and appreciate their essence.

KING OF CUPS

- RIVER • *Purpose – Compassion – Boundaries*

A river flows with purpose. On the level of atoms, each droplet contains a microscopic world and has a destiny — the ocean. Gravity pulls the river in one direction, even as the water evaporates or sustains plants and creatures along the way. A drop is magnified in this card, made large as a reminder of water's centrality to life. Circular and cyclical, water comes and goes, rises and falls; just as our emotions do.

IN A READING •

UPRIGHT: The *King of Cups* symbolises a person who is connected to their ever-changing emotions, and responsive to others, whilst also holding their own course. People turn to them in times of crisis. This is because they are both porous and boundaried. They help others whilst also knowing how to say 'no' in a compassionate yet firm way. Maybe this card reminds you of someone who is skilled at this, or you are working on this yourself. This card comes to you as encouragement — it's good to keep your needs in mind alongside giving care and attention to others.

REVERSED: Beware of guarding your emotional energy. A river only reaches the sea by meeting and merging with other rivers. Trust that you can handle change, and let new people into your life.

QUEEN OF CUPS

- HUMPBACK WHALE   • *Empathy – Courage – Acceptance*

A humpback whale is one of the largest mammals on the planet; she has blood, milk, and warmth in common with her land-borne siblings, including humans. She thrives in icy waters and fathoms-deep pressures, and her gentle presence in the ocean is a thing of wonder to any person lucky enough to witness her. Water is her home and her realm; she is magisterial within it.

IN A READING •

UPRIGHT: The *Queen of Cups* represents a person who feels things to their deepest degrees. Pure joy, pure pain, pure hope, pure sorrow. This isn't an easy way to live, but it makes this person very strong, and unusually accepting of all emotions. Her caring and creative imagination means that she is skilled at empathising with others, no matter what their situation is. The *Queen of Cups* appears as an inspiration — an invitation to appreciate this non-judgemental part of yourself, and its presence in those around you.

REVERSED: The deeper waters of your emotional life feel distant and inaccessible. There's a reason for that. Take care of yourself by swimming along the surface, noticing the here-and-now. Inhale, exhale — just be.

THE WANDS

The wand—or staff—in tarot symbolises energy and action. A staff enables an intrepid traveller to go farther; a wand enables the sorceress to perform amazing feats.

Often depicted with leaves bursting from the shaft, wands are generative, phallic, and suggestive of new life, new beginnings.

Inspiration and creativity are associated with the Wands. They are auspicious cards for anyone embarking on a challenging project, being ambitious in their career, or pursuing a particular passion.

Wands are paired with fire in tarot, with their wood providing a vital ingredient. Sometimes the energy of Wands leads to conflicts and thoughtlessness, but vitality is always present.

ACE OF WANDS

- STAFF • *Inspiration – Energy – Creativity*

The simple beginning — a wooden staff, there for the taking. Flowering plants tenderly grow in the direction of light and heat. The upright triangle is the alchemical symbol for fire, an emblem for movement, warmth, embers, and infernos. This is the realm of fire energy — taking action, setting forth, and being adventurous.

IN A READING •

UPRIGHT: All new endeavours begin with inspiration. The *Ace of Wands* heralds a moment of pure arrival: This is what I want to do. When you feel a creative impulse, act on it — take the first step, fan the first flame.

The earliest stage of creation is invisible to onlookers. And the process of bringing something into being—allowing the forces of reality to give it form—means that the end rarely resembles the dreamed-of beginning. That's fine;

that's good! Take the energy of the *Ace of Wands* and conjure with it. Your vision deserves life.

REVERSED: A block prevents you from acting on your dreams. This could be financial, practical, or psychological. Pay attention to this block and use your creative abilities to dissolve it.

TWO OF WANDS

- BRIDGE
- *Partnership – Opportunity – Intention*

Two figures meet at the crown of a monumental bridge. They have set out on their respective paths with the intention of getting somewhere — reaching the other side. In meeting on this fragile yet effective bridge, they are equals who share similar goals. Each can bring creative fire to a new project. And each is curious about what opportunities and possibilities are generated by leaving home and venturing out.

IN A READING

UPRIGHT: The *Two of Wands* relates to being in your comfort zone, and feeling ready to leave its orbit. Restlessness can become purposeful: Seek out an alliance with someone who inspires you, or experiment with trying out whatever is opposite to your default creative or professional instincts. Pursue any opportunities you notice, and accept the challenges that accompany them. Planned precariousness creates focus.

REVERSED: An established partnership is feeling a bit dull. Talk about what brought you together to begin with. Shift things by prioritising fun new experiences. Agree to take some risks together.

THREE OF WANDS

- MOUNTAIN • *Adventure – Ascent – Determination*

The highest peak of a mountain is a rarified environment, exposed to the sun's heat, the wildest winds, and dense canopies of cloud. Only a few plants and creatures can survive at such elevation, and human beings are not naturally well-equipped for it. To even briefly reach a summit requires tenacity and strength; an ability to plan and prepare, too. The exhilarating perspective gained is what makes it all worthwhile.

IN A READING •

UPRIGHT: Live adventurously, and aim high. Define success on your terms. When you climb a mountain alone, the route and pace are up to you, and your experience will be personal to you, too.

The *Three of Wands* is an auspicious card, and it sees your determined nature. Just as reaching great altitudes on foot involves sweat, burning muscles, and careful navigation, your ambition will challenge you as well as reward you. Envision your goal, and map out how you'll reach it.

REVERSED: The mountain inverted. Descend into the subterranean layers of your unconscious self — dreams, nightmares, memories. Quest for self-knowledge; observe how it shapes your daily decisions.

FOUR OF WANDS

- GARLAND
- *Celebration – Gathering – Holiday*

Four straight-standing wands are unified, and a garland of fresh flowers is the crowning glory. The flowers have been gathered for a happy and long-awaited day — a celebration. After a long winter, spring flowers arrive, ready to be deftly woven together into something special. Their beauty will only last the day. But they bring a touch of conscious and creative magic to the festivities at hand, and to whoever wears them.

IN A READING

UPRIGHT: The *Four of Wands* blesses you with revelry. Whatever pressures and stresses may be present for you, think about moments of real leisure within your reach … a public holiday or a trip to somewhere new; a party, a festival, or carnival. And any time or place where you fully disconnect from work. Notice the sweet things that togetherness and celebration make room for — headlong joys, inventive forms of self-expression, and spontaneous bursts of laughter.

REVERSED: Big family get-togethers or social gatherings can be hard when you're feeling out of sorts. What feels leisurely and enjoyable to you right now? Prioritise that where possible.

FIVE OF WANDS

- CHAINS • *Teamwork – Debate – Rivalry*

These interlocking metal chain links are rigid with tension. A padlock firmly secures the inner circle. There are tilted wands and upright wands — no unity. Disagreement and competition are the energising factors at play here, but it's resulting in a stalemate. Progress will only occur when there is a shift in alignment.

IN A READING

UPRIGHT: A tussle for power lies at the heart of the *Five of Wands*, but it's more of a skirmish than a battle. However, egos may get bruised, and unhelpful certainties may become more deeply rooted.

The fiery energy of the Wands suit can be both an asset and a hindrance to teamwork. A desire to 'win' may fuel your ability to argue for a particular outcome, but a win/lose mindset will damage a team effort. To unlock a tense situation, seek consensus on how to work together.

REVERSED: When you're part of a winning team, there's much to enjoy, but over time successes can grow stale. It's healthy to move on if so — the team will adapt and so will you.

SIX OF WANDS

- CHRYSANTHEMUMS
- *Success – Recognition – Celebration*

Chrysanthemums are associated with lasting vitality. When cut, a chrysanthemum flower stays fresh and bright for a long time. Because they endure so well, they are often given by mourners, acting as a comforting reminder of care once the funeral ends. Their most popular use, however, is for festive occasions — they can be threaded into abundant garlands, decorating celebratory events and celebrated people. Chrysanthemums suit both quiet moments and loud ones.

IN A READING

UPRIGHT: Celebration comes in many forms. Sometimes, the moment of recognition—the finish line, an awards ceremony, or a launch night—is very public. More often, triumph is a private event. When you achieve something you've worked hard for, mark your success. Buy yourself flowers. Propose a toast with friends. Do whatever makes you happy!

REVERSED: You're doing well, but you don't really *feel* like you're doing well. When you receive praise or reach a milestone, share the good news — others may help you make it feel real.

SEVEN OF WANDS

- WOLF   • *Struggle – Integrity – Resistance*

Wolves are pack animals, and so the idea of a lone wolf is very powerful. A lone wolf is unpredictable, perhaps even dangerous, now that it has dared to venture away from the social comforts and pressures of the wolf family. Lone wolves are oddities and exceptions, willing to accept being vulnerable to a riskier existence in exchange for independence.

IN A READING •

UPRIGHT: There are times when the prevailing ethos of a group is not only misguided, but actively harmful. Some people keep quiet when their concerns are unpopular or outvoted by the majority. But the *Seven of Wands* celebrates those who speak up against harm-doing, and demonstrate integrity through their actions.

It takes courage to say when something is wrong if nobody else seems to share your perspective. It will feel lonely and alienating at first, but your resistance to an oppressive norm will help you find a new wolf-pack, where honesty is valued over suppression and conformity.

REVERSED: Hold your own counsel. In a destructive dynamic, being honest may make you vulnerable, and your words may well be twisted against you. Absent yourself quietly; speaking your truth can happen when you are safe.

EIGHT OF WANDS

- FIST • *Resolve – Momentum – Conclusion*

Energy has a trajectory — the rising arc upwards, the peaking focus, and the final flurry of completion. The raised fist symbolises bringing together energy and gathering strength in readiness for a conclusion. A major impact is in the offing, and the balanced wands, the mirrored orbs, and the tapering circles all call forth firmness of purpose.

IN A READING •

UPRIGHT: Even passion projects can become exhausting. Your energies are flagging, and so the *Eight of Wands* counsels you to take heart — you have already gathered your resources, and you know what you are trying to accomplish. Being tired is a sign of how much work you have already completed, so don't let that work go to waste. Pour your remaining energies into the project, and bring it to a satisfying conclusion. You're nearly there!

REVERSED: A project you left unfinished weighs on your mind. Take it as a sign of how prolific you are — you do many things, and complete most of them. It's likely that your energy for this project went slack for a reason.

NINE OF WANDS

- DEER   • *Fatigue – Injury – Tenacity*

A wounded hart—or young male deer—has been brought down by a hunter's arrow. Deer are representatives of our innocent, sensitive selves, vulnerable to the predatory manoeuvres of others. This deer is forced to pause, to acknowledge its injury. It may rest and recover undisturbed, or it may be discovered and pushed to defend itself, through either fight or flight.

IN A READING •

UPRIGHT: Fighting every battle that comes your way is a sure way to lose touch with yourself. Take the time to tend to any deeper pain you're experiencing. Try not to minimise it or run away from it — respond to your pain with care. You may feel defenceless or feeble when you are not 'being productive' or engaging with some wider struggle. But exhaustion will not cure you. Remember that healing and true persistence are enabled by rest.

REVERSED: After retreating for a while, long-term stillness becomes stiffness. How might you begin your return to the fray?

TEN OF WANDS

- BURNING HOUSE • *Burn-out – Obsession – Urgency*

This house is on fire, and instant and intense action is required if anything is to be salvaged. Yet the all-consuming power of fire can be mesmerising. Plenty of fuel has gone into these flames, and plenty more will soon be used. No one can rest easy until every cinder has been doused. And even then, there is the work of sifting through the ash and wreckage.

IN A READING •

UPRIGHT: The *Ten of Wands* means that you need respite from whatever is consuming you. Burnout occurs when you're left to fulfil crucial yet overwhelming tasks. And there's no point in sacrificing yourself on the fire. Instead, trust that you have the power to respond effectively. Be assertive: Enlist help, attend to the crisis, and be mindful of your health. Let others play their part alongside you.

REVERSED: Things feel relatively peaceful right now; in fact, your tiredness may well be boredom. Offer help to a friend, or set yourself a new goal.

PAGE OF WANDS

- SALAMANDER • *Apprenticing – Adaptability – Self-Assurance*

Salamanders are amphibious creatures, able to live on land and in water. Ancient Greeks believed that they could pass through fire unharmed too, and in Greek their name roughly translates to 'fire lizard'. It's not true that salamanders have an affinity with fire, but it is a fact that they are survivors. As a species, they have existed for millions of years, and as individuals, their lifespans can exceed a century. Whatever myths spring up around them, salamanders endure.

IN A READING •

UPRIGHT: When learning something new, your ability is measured by the progress you make, rather than by your reputation. You don't need to devote energy towards being the 'best in class'. It's fine to learn slowly, or make mistakes; it's part of learning. Your fear of failure is the real fire you must pass through in order to keep going. When shame comes knocking, think about how far you've already come, and be proud of your commitment to learning.

REVERSED: When you seek out feedback, it can be hard to hear criticism — especially when you know it's accurate! Stick with it. Over time, your tolerance to critique will build, and your performance will improve.

KNIGHT OF WANDS

• LIONESS   • *Enthusiasm – Charm – Unreliability*

No longer a cub and not yet an adult, this young lioness commands attention. Eyes full of flames and ears pricked, her direct focus is not to be doubted. Neither is her confident energy, which is sure to help her bring down plenty of prey — but only when her skills match her keenness. She may tire easily, and let things get away from her, but she'll be captivating to watch, no matter what.

IN A READING •

UPRIGHT: The *Knight of Wands* symbolises a person who brings energy and enthusiasm to whatever they try their hand at. It's enjoyable to be around them, as their attitude makes them highly attractive. They may be a great asset to a project, or a charismatic friend or lover, but the *Knight of Wands* also contains unpredictability. When this card appears, there's a chance things will go well, and there's also a chance you'll be left empty-handed. Appreciate the fire this person brings, without expecting more.

REVERSED: Don't bank on someone's potential if what you really require is reliability. Avoid frustration by seeking what you need.

KING OF WANDS

- KEYS • *Dynamic – Unconventional – Practical*

Echoing the keys-to-the-universe quality of *The Emperor (4)*, these two keys are bound to open important doors. The *King of Wands* encapsulates the leadership aspect of the fiery Wands suit — the ability to act upon reality, creatively and with ambition. The confidence and skill represented by the Wands are expansive, unlocking new possibilities.

IN A READING

UPRIGHT: When you take a daydream and use your skills to make it tangible, a thing that exists in the world, you are embodying the *King of Wands*. Amplify your inner creative, and be authoritative about prioritising work and pursuits that you feel passionate about. Treat your abilities as keys to your future — which doors will they open up for you?

REVERSED: Self-doubt is like a rusted key, creating friction and drag. Oil your progress through action: Ignore the fearful, 'sensible' part of your brain, over and over, until you've proven to yourself that you can do this.

QUEEN OF WANDS

- SUNFLOWER • *Confidence – Character – Zest*

Sunflowers are well named, their wide faces following the path of the Sun itself. They convert every bit of light and warmth and soil into strong, bristled stems, spiral-patterned seed disks, and fiery yellow-orange petals. A sunflower is a source of pollen to insects, and food to people as well as birds. It also catches the eye, without apology. Sunflowers give everything back tenfold, with a joyful aura.

IN A READING •

UPRIGHT: This sunflower symbolises a confident person who has a warm, friendly personality. Their radiance is immediate and impossible to hide. Like a sunflower, the person represented by the *Queen of Wands* is dynamic — they actively lean towards the light. This person looks for the good in people, favours action over deliberation, and is skilled at offering creative solutions to difficult situations. The *Queen of Wands* appears in your reading as inspiration; let her generous, life-affirming spirit help you bloom.

REVERSED: When you feel down or insecure, it can be daunting to be around someone so cheerful. Trust that they are kind, as well as extroverted. Let them see where you're at, so that they can be vulnerable in turn.

THE SWORDS

Cutting and cool to the touch, the Swords symbolise thought, knowledge, and reason in tarot. They celebrate curiosity and the pleasures of thinking and learning. However, they are a challenging suit; when swords appear in a reading, a tough decision may need to be made, or you may benefit from rethinking how you approach your situation.

A sword is only useful if it is sharp and well-balanced. Continually honing and testing your critical faculties leads to good decision-making. Without careful consideration, it can be difficult to act fairly and wisely.

An upright sword symbolises justice, clean and true. A tilted sword indicates indecision. Downward-pointing swords refer to problems that stem from being 'in our heads' too much — anxiety, fear, or limiting beliefs.

The Swords are linked to the element of air — like thoughts themselves, air is essential to us, yet almost intangible. Crisp, cloudless air corresponds to clear thinking; cloudy, stormy imagery relates to confusion and turmoil.

ACE OF SWORDS

• SWORD   • *Inspiration – Clarity – Truth*

Clouds part to reveal a sword in a position of perfect readiness, upright and primed for action. Flowering tendrils spill out of a lock, and its key is close by. The sword is inanimate, hard, sharp, cold, and commanding; its blade and intricately studded hilt are both products of precise and sustained attention. In contrast, the flowers grow as a matter of course, their tender stems animated by life.

IN A READING •

UPRIGHT: Curiosity, good decision-making, clear thinking, and a love of justice; the invigorating aspects of the Swords suit are all represented by this shining Ace. This card celebrates the clarity of your perceptions and the complexity of your psyche. The *Ace of Swords* encourages you to be decisive, to learn something new, and to speak your truth. Give oxygen to your ideas and watch them come alive in the world.

REVERSED: Second-guessing yourself indicates that you no longer trust your inner logic. Allow yourself to do things differently—make some 'mistakes'—and let that guide you back towards self-knowledge.

TWO OF SWORDS

- WALL • *Obstruction – Pressure – Inertia*

A slab of stone can be used to build a wall, or to seal a tomb. The solidity of this gravestone-like structure keeps things apart, working both as a shelter and a blockade. Its heft is also hard to shift, and potentially crushing. Manoeuvring such a heavy slab requires energy and ingenuity. Protective swords must be uncrossed to begin that work. Stars and space and weightlessness lie behind this stone — are they worth reaching?

IN A READING •

UPRIGHT: Inaction is a more active state than it seems. Often, immobility is caused by the presence of an oppressive force. Examine your current situation and identify any feelings of stuckness. Maybe you feel burdened with a big decision, or it feels like you're the only one holding the fort. Or maybe you are tired of maintaining an 'acceptable' persona — a façade.

When struggling with something intractable, be fluid and playful in your problem-solving to generate new options. Something dazzling awaits you on the other side of the wall.

REVERSED: You've tried to overcome a frustrating situation, and yet you've hit the same old block. Acceptance may serve you better for the time being; as circumstances naturally change, new energies and strategies will come to you.

THREE OF SWORDS

- STORM   • *Heartbreak – Betrayal – Disappointment*

A mighty storm rages in the sky while three swords bear down into a single point. Their combined downward pressure concentrates the injury they create, and compounds the sense of misfortune. Pain and the desire to escape pain are equally present.

IN A READING •

UPRIGHT: The *Three of Swords* recognises the deep mental distress triggered by love gone wrong. The storm represents your inner turmoil, while the swords represent the causes of your pain. The appearance of this card suggests that now is a good time to grapple with what hurts you. Each sword corresponds to a person or an element of your situation; let yourself feel whatever comes up when you think of them. After the storm passes, breathe deeply. You are making space for clarity, healing, and decisions that take you in a positive direction.

REVERSED: The storm feels distant — but it's unlikely to have passed. You may be numbing yourself in response to ongoing difficult conditions. Until the clouds disperse, a clear vision of the future may feel remote, too.

FOUR OF SWORDS

- EYES • *Rest – Pause – Sanctuary*

The wide-open eyes of a young person look up at the sky. They direct their attention to the air, the stars, the clouds, the heavens. The occupations of everyday life are not in focus, and their swords all lie flat. This is a moment of calm, relaxed, free-flowing thought. A dreaming mind can create respite from thin air.

IN A READING

UPRIGHT: It's time to rest. But being busy is a socially accepted defence against bids on your attention, such as a person or obligation you don't wish to make time for. The *Four of Swords* is compassionate to your reasons for keeping busy, whilst also saying it's restorative to seek out peace and put down your swords. Ignore life's demands for a spell, and tend to your spirit. Let daydreams tumble through your mind.

REVERSED: Pressure to be productive is causing you stress, rather than helping you get things done. Address the situation with whoever is setting the pace — whether that is an employer, a client, or your own inner critic.

FIVE OF SWORDS

- SCISSORS   • *Contest – Severance – Distance*

Scissors smoothly cut up what is whole, and separate what has been woven together. Division comes easily with a sharp pair of blades; the act of cutting something into many pieces is simple and absolute. Here, five swords are set carefully apart. After a messy and heated disagreement, there can be a need for neat, cool, clear distance. There is also an absence of mending tools, like a needle and thread, that could repair this kind of fallout.

IN A READING •

UPRIGHT: The *Five of Swords* refers to the aftermath of a conflict or contest where there are distinct winners and losers. Rivalry tends to deepen your understanding of both yourself and those who challenge you. Tensions have run high, and you've either won or lost. How do you feel now? What has this battle revealed? Is distance helping, or hurting?

REVERSED: Subtle conflict — the unspoken, unresolved kind. Beware of resentment, passive-aggression, and score-settling. Have an honest conversation with the person you feel antagonism towards.

SIX OF SWORDS

- BOAT • *Departure – Homesickness – Travel*

A small-yet-sturdy boat awaits passengers. A seabird perches on the prow, symbolic of spiritual guidance (birds are messengers for the gods), and also of escape and flight. This bird is a trusty guide, able to navigate land, water, and air. Clouds float around the boat, representing uncertainty; the vessel's route is not visible, nor is its destination.

IN A READING

UPRIGHT: A card for leaving — and setting out in search of new possibilities. The *Six of Swords* supports you in saying goodbye to an old situation. It makes no promises about what the future holds for you; the message of this card is to move forward, even if you feel homesick or unsure about the journey. Equally, you don't need to wait to be fully 'over' a conflict, trauma, or bereavement before starting again. Travel, trips, and seeking out new experiences will help lessen the immediacy of past pain.

REVERSED: Returning to a place you chose to leave behind will bring back old feelings. Remember that you can change your part of the script by doing things differently this time.

SEVEN OF SWORDS

- LOCKED BOX • *Secrecy – Deception – Self-Interest*

An invitingly decorated trunk is ready to be unlocked. The flowers growing from the keyhole hint at treasures—or loot—within. But the row of swords laid tip to tail feel spiked and dangerous: a warning. In the story of Pandora's box, all the sins of the world are unleashed by opening up that which should remain firmly closed. Proceed with caution.

IN A READING •

UPRIGHT: It's smart to mistrust others at times. Scams happen; lies and sins of omission can materialise in relationships, and the deepest betrayals emerge from well-established bonds. When you sense that something is not quite right, or perhaps too good to be true, it's healthy to scan for signs of deception. Act with your best interests in mind if your suspicions prove to be well-founded. Sometimes, your own behaviour may foster mistrust, too; try not to take it personally or over-explain. You're entitled to be private, and it's not necessary to be open-handed in every scenario.

REVERSED: If you are devoting large amounts of energy to protecting your assets, or acquiring more-more-more, it may be time to reassess what's truly at risk.

EIGHT OF SWORDS

- HURT BIRD • *Limitation – Stress – Self-Sabotage*

A songbird is pierced by a downward-slanting arrow, symbolising an airborne spirit being swiftly returned to earth. Small birds are fast-moving, fast-living creatures, constantly vulnerable to danger, and constantly flitting away from it. The heartbeat of a songbird is rapid, and easily snuffed out. Four braces of swords block out the open skies.

IN A READING •

UPRIGHT: Symbolic of feeling trapped, the *Eight of Swords* relates to an anxious mental state combined with restrictive circumstances. Fragile, fluttering energy can quickly become panic and desperation. You feel thwarted, but your escape strategy is not delivering freedom — yet. Try not to fling yourself headlong at your problems. Sit yourself down and assess your position, calmly and firmly.

REVERSED: Free-falling into familiar anxieties robs you of joy. Halt the spiral by spending even a small part of your day in nature. Pause any actions that could be described as 'frantic'.

NINE OF SWORDS

- TEARS • *Helplessness – Sorrow – Despair*

An eye looks out from within a sacred flower. It sees the sorrows of the world and does not blink or shut out what is happening. Instead, it cries, the tears flowing forth, their salty softness meeting the unforgiving swords that seem to gather below, threatening the undefended eye.

IN A READING •

UPRIGHT: Horror and atrocity weave their way into your psyche, and your awareness of them is painful. You do what you can to make things right, but it doesn't seem to be enough. Maybe you have high hopes that things will get better, but when they don't, despair follows. To avoid bitterness, express your grief and rage as fully as you can, then return to the discipline of hope. Bear witness and let yourself be moved to act again.

REVERSED: Holding your emotions in check is considerate when others are suffering badly, but do seek an outlet for your strong feelings — they exist for a reason.

TEN OF SWORDS

- SWAN
- *Woundedness – Catastrophising – Drama*

A swan coils in on itself as it perches upon a nest of swords. Embracing adversity in a painful situation can be an excellent coping strategy. But in the long term, is self-sacrifice comfortable, healthy, or necessary? This swan has opted to make these ten sharp blades into a bed — but it could choose differently.

IN A READING

UPRIGHT: The *Ten of Swords* recognises an aggrieved part of you. You feel attacked — and your wounded reaction adds a whole new layer of drama to the situation. But being a martyr only pushes people away. Sleeping on a bed of swords helps no one, least of all you!

A subtext of this card is that the script can always be changed. You have agency, more than you realise! Identifying the part you are playing in fuelling negative dynamics releases you from feeling like a helpless victim. Your role may well be the only thing you have control over — so change it up and see what happens.

REVERSED: Are you under-reacting to something important, due to its overwhelming nature? Addressing your situation in small, practical steps will help to make it less daunting.

PAGE OF SWORDS

- WINDOW • *Learning – Curiosity – Eagerness*

A window is a threshold, allowing light and air into sheltered interiors. From within, it protects you whilst also framing the world outside. When you look into a window, you glimpse into someone's private experience. The transparent two-way quality of a window allows for anticipation, discovery, and previews of what is to come, all within safe confines.

IN A READING

UPRIGHT: When you approach an unfamiliar subject with openness and an earnest, unself-conscious interest in learning, you embody 'beginner's mind', a Zen concept also referred to as *shoshin*. Have fun learning something entirely new, and notice its effect on your relationship with the world. Curiosity is transformative! Unshutter the windows of your psyche and welcome in currents of fresh air, from a vantage point that shelters you from any stormy weather.

REVERSED: It's natural to plateau at times when learning something new. Don't worry too much — you're just consolidating what you've already absorbed. Keep going and a new vista will open up eventually.

KNIGHT OF SWORDS

- BRAIN • *Perception – Reasoning – Limitation*

The human brain contains billions of neurons and trillions of connections. Its electrochemical reactions enable us to learn and perceive, and create infinite amazing scenarios — many of which we can translate into reality. Even so, our brains make plenty of mistakes, and like every other organ, it can be affected by illness and injury. Fallibility is part of reasoning; the trick is to make peace with that. In tarot, a tilting sword is symbolic of uncertainty, of not having all the facts.

IN A READING •

UPRIGHT: The *Knight of Swords* gives you an opportunity to reflect on your relationship to 'rightness', 'wrongness', and the state of not knowing. Uncertainty is unsettling, and hard to bear for long; but absolute certainty dulls perception, and can have a bludgeoning effect on others.

Something weighs heavily on your mind — a big decision, a complex scenario. Consider the facts available to you with extra care before reaching towards a conclusion. Even after you make up your mind, some doubts will remain — and that is okay. It's healthy to be able to live with a degree of uncertainty. Take calculated risks when you judge your circumstances to be favourable enough, rather than fully perfect.

REVERSED: You're uncomfortably aware of having made a mistake. Instead of ruminating on it, turn your mind to making things right and formulating a satisfying repair.

KING OF SWORDS

- BUTTERFLY • *Intelligence – Facility – Leadership*

Creatures of the air are often charismatic, and butterflies especially so. Clever on a DNA level, butterfly-wing patterns act as disguises, warnings, and illusions. Those fragile, almost weightless wings are strong enough to withstand thousand-mile migrations, and butterflies dance lightly through heat and storms to reach their roosting sites. Each butterfly starts earth-bound, as an egg, then a caterpillar, then a chrysalis — flight only comes with maturity.

IN A READING •

UPRIGHT: The *King of Swords* refers to a person with an original mind. They are inventive, and they search for knowledge with precision and curiosity. In a leadership role, their intelligence is inspiring, and they'll challenge you at times, pushing you to evolve beyond habitual thinking.

To channel the *King of Swords*, revisit a long-held opinion or idea that once felt sharp, but has started to feel stale and cliché. Consider new angles. Lead others by sharing your thought processes, mistakes and all, and respond nimbly to shifting circumstances.

REVERSED: When decision-making, notice weighty emotions—like shame, fear, or pride—that could be clouding your judgement. Try to set these aside, and act in service of the outcome you hope to achieve.

QUEEN OF SWORDS

- ELDER • *Wisdom – Depth – Experience*

The bright eyes of an elder queen meet your gaze. The broad span of her life contains whole eras, hundreds of thousands of conversations, a million actions. She's played many roles, and felt every emotion you could name. Her self-possession is hard-won, gleaned from difficult experiences that she made a conscious decision to heal from rather than pass on. This queen embodies equanimity—an 'equal mind'—and an open, intelligent spirit.

IN A READING •

UPRIGHT: The *Queen of Swords* is a mentor you can turn to when you need a clear, sharp eye to look over your decisions. Having weathered her own challenges, she is empathetic, yet not indulgent; she won't sugarcoat her advice. She expects you to act with integrity. There is an irreverent side to this queen — because she has seen suffering, she also knows when not to take things too seriously. The *Queen of Swords* is here to help you make sense of life, and laugh at the absurdity of it all, too.

REVERSED: Not every elder is wise. Someone can live for a long time without ever developing self-knowledge or compassion. If an elder lectures you without showing insight into your situation, by all means, ignore their advice.

THE PENTACLES

In the simplest terms, the Pentacles are the coins of tarot. They represent security and resourcefulness — whatever it is that you require on a practical level. Shelter, warmth, and food are universally important things, and the Pentacles suit recognises their significance.

The coins in this deck bear the insignia of an animal closely linked with abundance — the hare. Like the hare, these coins are designed to be in motion. Symbolism relating to exchange, storage, and effort can be seen across the cards of this suit.

When Pentacles appear in your reading, explore your relationship to need, productivity, and provision. Work is very much in the realm of Pentacles.

The alchemic symbol for salt, which represents the earth beneath our feet, is tied to the Pentacles. This is because feeling stable, secure, and at peace often involves being grounded and taking root. Connect with what is tangible — your body, your possessions, your resources. The Pentacles affirm what is within reach.

ACE OF PENTACLES

- HARE-COIN • *Resources – Competence – Plenty*

The majestic hare stamped on this golden coin is a blessing on a blessing — in tarot, a Pentacle coin represents having something that is of value, something worthwhile. And the hare is a powerful symbol of energy, abundance, and vitality. New leaves and flowers frame the hare's field, where it lives close to the ground. Beneath the hare-coin, the elemental symbol for earth points downwards, signifying rootedness and practicality.

IN A READING

UPRIGHT: The *Ace of Pentacles* heralds the beginning of a prosperous season — now is the time to scatter seeds and tend to what grows. Be resourceful and generous with yourself; invest in whatever you need in order to get started. The efforts you make now will bring many kinds of growth; you'll become more skilled, you'll figure out practical solutions to problems, and your self-confidence will increase, too. Cherish the relationships that give you a feeling of stability, and let them inspire you to set rewarding new endeavours in motion.

REVERSED: It's good to be diligent about providing for yourself and those around you, but it's important to relax, as well. Plan a day off, and do something that you enjoy.

TWO OF PENTACLES

• INFINITY • *Flow – Focus – Occupation*

Two hare-coins mirror each other in perfect balance, linked by the grounding energy of the earth sign, a bisected downward-pointing triangle. The symmetry of the currency symbolises a kind of mathematical wonder that can be found through work — in the process of focusing closely on a task and performing brilliantly at it. No energy is diverted away from the goal; all actions flow smoothly towards it.

IN A READING •

UPRIGHT: Your attention is a precious commodity! When it is keenly focused on your work, you'll experience a kind of busy peace. As you become more skilled, learn from your mistakes, and produce better results, you'll enjoy work more and more. Your efforts become a virtuous and infinitely evolving loop. When the *Two of Pentacles* appears in a reading, it suggests that work is to be your prime concern — and that it will richly reward you, both emotionally and financially.

REVERSED: Beware of wasting time by fixating on unresolvable issues. Consider your overarching goals. Communicate what you aren't able to do, and what you are.

THREE OF PENTACLES

- BUFFALO   • *Collaboration – Craft – Alliance*

Three buffalo move as a group. They are united in purpose and direction, and their combined presence is a force to be reckoned with. Buffalo are strong, gentle creatures, able to carry great loads and accomplish feats of endurance. They are naturally sociable, too. Peaceable camaraderie is part of their gift for labour.

IN A READING •

UPRIGHT: Working within a dynamic team is a life-affirming experience. When you form an alliance with people of complementary and diverse talents, your skills are bound to shine brightly, and you'll have the same effect on others. On a practical note, by welcoming collaboration and pulling together, you can accomplish far more within a team than you would do alone. And on a personal level, the bonds you forge when working closely with someone can be as meaningful as any romance or friendship.

REVERSED: Enjoyable teamwork can distract you from your craft. Trust your abilities outside of a group context; balance your schedule with some solo work.

FOUR OF PENTACLES

- CRACKED MIRROR   • *Worry – Materialism – Insecurity*

A broken mirror signifies seven years of bad luck. The deeper meaning here is that placing great emphasis on intrinsically fragile and impermanent objects is a recipe for disappointment. Money buys many forms of comfort and luxury, but these do not necessarily guarantee contentment. Prizing items that can easily be damaged, lost, or depreciated is a risky business.

IN A READING •

UPRIGHT: The *Four of Pentacles* is a card that reflects money worries and high concern with material goods. The jagged reflection offered by a cracked mirror suggests that not all feelings of financial insecurity are grounded in reality. Money matters, but it can also immobilise you and rob you of your creative energies, your loving spirit, and your good humour. Examine your relationship to acquiring things. How are your instincts helping you, or hindering you?

REVERSED: Practise letting things go — if you have things that take up space but rarely get used, consider selling them or giving them away. The objects will have a new lease of life, and so will you.

FIVE OF PENTACLES

- YELLOW CARNATION
- *Rejection – Need – Exclusion*

A yellow carnation is symbolic of rejection and sorrow. Sometimes sent as a bouquet that signifies apology, they are flowers associated with attempts to make things right. Here, the carnations are bordered by a black square, which is overlapped by a small white-and-black disc. The square excludes the dark half of the circle. The carnations are a reparative gesture, but their impact doesn't extend far.

IN A READING •

UPRIGHT: Rejection has cumulative effects on the psyche, and systemic exclusion from society and its resources amounts to violence. When you experience great need, you tend to be in a position of vulnerability. Ask for help from people you trust. Be alert to anyone who tries to use your suffering to their advantage. You are capable of getting through tough times.

REVERSED: When making amends for an injustice, listen to the actual and stated needs of the mistreated person or group. Avoid self-serving, self-soothing gestures; provide the requested material help instead.

SIX OF PENTACLES

- CORNUCOPIA • *Generosity – Surplus – Charity*

A flow of money spirals out of a horn of plenty, otherwise known as a cornucopia. Cornucopias are associated with fantastic abundance — they only ever half-contain their spillage of good things. Here, the beneficence loops outwards and spins back. Liberal circulation of wealth is a virtue.

IN A READING

UPRIGHT: Charity is a complex thing, loaded with positive and negative associations. The *Six of Pentacles* invites you to consider your relationship to giving and receiving. What rules and conditions do you apply to yourself, and others, in situations where generosity is called for? Give what you can and enjoy what you have. Life is short!

REVERSED: Costs can spiral easily when times are good. When you hit a rough patch, balancing your outgoings against your income will keep you steady until things get better again.

SEVEN OF PENTACLES

- FROG • *Progress – Review – Aspiration*

Frogs represent betweenness. Their smooth, slippery skin draws oxygen from both water and air, and they move through many forms to reach their maturity, from spawn to tadpole to vertebrate. In myth, they are often magical, transforming into human beings.

A frog's athleticism and adaptability are apparent whether it is underwater or venturing beyond its pool. This tree frog is on the ascendant, and is limber and focused in its pursuit of new heights. Not every coin is in place yet, but they soon will be.

IN A READING ·

UPRIGHT: Pause to assess where you are in relation to your highest goals. Put small tasks and your to-do list to one side, and think big. The *Seven of Pentacles* suggests that you are on your way to realising your ambitions. Keep in mind the version of yourself that you intend to become, because it's a vision that only you can truly know. Once you've taken stock of your current vantage point, keep climbing — you'll get there.

REVERSED: Existing in a state of 'becoming' can be tiresome. Try to notice and enjoy the special privileges of being in a liminal state, before the responsibilities of a more 'fixed' identity become yours.

EIGHT OF PENTACLES

- HAMMER
- *Determination – Industry – Devotion*

The blunt weight of a lump hammer requires strength to pick up, and force to use. Without the application of effort, such a hammer is near useless; when handled by an expert with confidence and focus, it delivers clear results. Using such a tool is laborious but ultimately effective.

IN A READING •

UPRIGHT: When you reach the crunch point of a project, you're going to feel it. Big demands are being made on your time, energy, and resources. It's time to lean into the challenge and commit fully to the next task, and the next one, and the next — until it is done. This level of work will test your passion and willpower, and it'll be incredibly satisfying to complete.

REVERSED: You're struggling to finish a project. You are not a machine — rest, seek support from those you are working with, and aim for completion, not perfection.

NINE OF PENTACLES

- RAINBOW • *Independence – Abundance – Stability*

The gorgeousness of a rainbow is a fleeting event, and it promises good fortune to all who witness it. Rainbows follow stormy weather, and their appearance announces the arrival of fresh, sparkling light. The ground has been well watered by rains, and now new growth can occur. The neatly aligned coins symbolise the pleasures of being orderly. They are a reminder that a rainbow's colourful blessing only appears when certain factors make it possible.

IN A READING •

UPRIGHT: The *Nine of Pentacles* is a lucky card, evoking a period of stability and good fortune. Having enough money to do as you like is a powerful thing, and your financial independence is a worthy goal. When you protect or increase your personal funds with this in mind, you create auspicious conditions for yourself. This card affirms your enjoyment of self-reliance, and your ability to take care of your financial wellbeing.

REVERSED: Visible good fortune brings its own costs, such as anxieties around how to enjoy it or share it, without attracting envy or false friends. Wealth in any form can create spiritual struggles that are hidden from view.

TEN OF PENTACLES

- CONTACT • *Exchange – Prosperity – Connection*

Two people reach out to hold hands. There is a relaxed feeling between their hands — a mutual desire for brief contact, free from the need to grasp or drag. Each hand has a coin at its centre, symbolising a happy sense of self-provision, and also an openness to exchange and giving freely. These two individuals feel generous and trusting towards each other, and coins abound around them.

IN A READING

UPRIGHT: The *Ten of Pentacles* shows us that friendly exchange creates a sense of confidence, in yourself and in others. Both earning and spending money can be sources of satisfaction, and help foster community. This card celebrates the abundant and ordinary human interactions that are part of everyday life — the simple exchange of words, energy, and eye contact you have with customers, shopkeepers, clients, employees, and employers. Small gestures of generosity can lift your spirits and brighten someone else's day. When you approach transactions with warmth, it will be returned to you.

REVERSED: Everyone else seems to have so much, and money seems to flow all around. You feel shut out and shortchanged. Be proactive. Prioritise interactions where your worth is rewarded.

PAGE OF PENTACLES

- RABBIT • *Planning – Luck – Excitement*

A white rabbit leaps over his mirror image, who symbolises a subconscious part — a part that shadows him and grounds him. A white rabbit is lucky; superstition links him with new beginnings and new moons. Though rabbits are of the earth and naturally feel safest in their underground warrens, this rabbit is airborne, daring … willing to take a risk!

IN A READING

UPRIGHT: Luck is on your side, and taking a risk now could bring about a positive change for you. Consider your current situation and challenge yourself to pursue a possibility that feels charged and exciting. Can you make more of your existing networks and resources? The *Page of Pentacles* has a fizzy, optimistic energy that empowers your most agile and go-getting self to embark upon a bold new venture.

REVERSED: You feel protective of your resources and have no desire to take risks. Trust your instincts — just as feeling lucky is a form of intuition, your caution is likely well-founded.

KNIGHT OF PENTACLES

- WATERWHEEL • *Industry – Predictability – Constance*

A mighty waterwheel turns and turns, effortlessly creating energy and power for its attendant mill. Its movements are predictable, and whether it moves fast or slow, it is reliable and productive. Though it goes nowhere, this wheel is an essential starting point for many resources. Above all, it is a symbol of industry.

IN A READING •

UPRIGHT: Steadiness is a quality that yields its rewards over time. The *Knight of Pentacles* represents a person who (or part of your personality that) tends to get on with things in an unshowy fashion, like a waterwheel fixed in place. This slow, consistent quality can feel routine, even soporific, but the results of this kind of labour are well worth the wait. A waterwheel ensures that grain becomes flour, and that flour becomes bread. Grinding away is not just useful, it is essential.

REVERSED: You feel dull and disconnected from the reasons for your labour. Revisit the original purpose of the work you have undertaken. Rest and reflect, and favour gradual progress over frantic outputs.

KING OF PENTACLES

- **PEACOCK** • *Assurance – Fortune – Grace*

An albino peacock stands with great poise. Being a male of his species, his magnificent tail feathers cascade behind him. In his case, their absence of pigment suggests both humility and transparency. Though this peacock lacks the flashing green-blue-gold 'eyes' of a typical peacock feather, he still stands out. His unusual colouring means he is extra-visible, in fact, and he attracts attention wherever he goes. He accepts this reality without seeking to change himself.

IN A READING •

UPRIGHT: The *King of Pentacles* shows us how good fortune can shape a person's character for the better. Think of someone whose approach to financial wellbeing feels healthy and successful. Confident of their own ability to get by, they are generous without being deliberately showy. They are practical and treat money (their own and other people's) with respect. Consider their attributes, and take inspiration from their example.

REVERSED: Lavish generosity—or expectations of it—can dictate the terms of a relationship. This creates a barrier to true connection. Low-cost activities are great equalisers.

QUEEN OF PENTACLES

- SHE-GOAT • *Vitality – Provision – Canniness*

This goat is wise to the ways of the world and confident in her ability to navigate it. Her horns give her an air of devilishness, but her true character is direct and practical. She enjoys life as it comes, and doesn't fuss over the details. Goats are sure-footed, thick-skinned, and unbounded by the niceties of convention. They take care of themselves very well.

IN A READING

UPRIGHT: The *Queen of Pentacles* is here as an inspiration for you. She may represent someone you know, or an aspect of yourself. She embodies hardy practicality, and an ability to survive and thrive even when conditions are unfavourable. There's a wayward aspect to any goat, and this one encourages you to put down the rulebook and do things your way, without prioritising what others will think. Feel at home in your skin, and embrace your particular circumstances. Be, do, live, enjoy.

REVERSED: Your strong preferences are leading you to be combative to an unnecessary degree. Review your need to be in control.

ABOUT THE AUTHOR

SUKI FERGUSON is a writer living in London, UK.

The Symbolic Tarot is the third collaboration between her and Ana Novaes — together they wrote and illustrated *Nova Witch Tarot* (Blue Angel Publishing, 2024), a tarot deck for newbies aged 10 and upwards. Before that, they created the book *Young Oracle Tarot* (Quarto, 2022), a young person's guide to the cards. Available worldwide, *Young Oracle Tarot* has been translated into six languages. Suki is also the author of the children's book *Astrologica: An Encyclopedia of Myths and Legends from the Planets, Stars and Skies* (Quarto, 2025).

Suki reads tarot online for people around the world under the name Mirror Tarot. Her practice is reflective and interactive. Each reading centres on holding a therapeutic space where the client feels alive to fresh insight, and supported to connect with their own wisdom.

Of all the cards in tarot, the one Suki appreciates the most is *The Fool*. Like the Fool, she loves to say yes to life's twists and turns, just to see what will happen next.

www.sukiferguson.co.uk • @mirrortarot

ABOUT THE ARTIST

ANA NOVAES is a Brazilian artist based in São Paulo, active in the market since 2015 with publications worldwide, including *Soul Mirror Oracle*, *Nova Witch Tarot*, *Feminine Myths Oracle*, *Tarot of Secrets*, and *Soul Reflections Tarot* with Blue Angel Publishing. She explores the collective unconscious through symbols and images that evoke dreams waiting to be deciphered. Her focus is on feminine figures, aiming to create and bring new perspectives and representations to these images, far from the male gaze. Novaes' creations exist between the conscious and unconscious worlds, between reality and dreams, establishing worlds we can explore with greater depth and without fear.

Learn more at **ananovaes.art**

ALSO AVAILABLE FROM BLUE ANGEL®

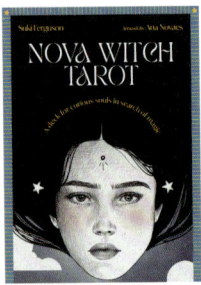

NOVA WITCH TAROT
A deck for curious souls in search of magic
Suki Ferguson • Artwork by Ana Novaes

Nova Witch Tarot is a captivating deck tailored for young hearts and those new to tarot. These 78 cards and colour guidebook are your trusted allies, helping you dance through life's twists and turns with empathy and self-love. Illuminate the countless facets of your being while discovering hidden potential and unexpected paths into the future.

78 Cards & Guidebook Set • ISBN: 978-1-922574-05-3

ALSO AVAILABLE FROM BLUE ANGEL®

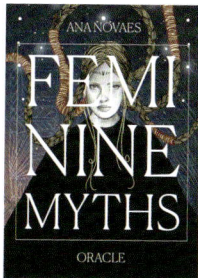

FEMININE MYTHS ORACLE
Ana Novaes

In this boldly illustrated oracle, feminine deities across many cultures have been uniquely reimagined with a surrealist twist to inspire your multi-faceted gifts. Receive guidance from these all-seeing, shapeshifting beings, who share the mythic stories of ancient Greece, Ireland, Haiti, Yorubaland, Japan and beyond. Each card's messenger brings primordial wisdom to help you navigate towards the visions of your soul.

50 Cards & Guidebook Set • ISBN: 978-1-922574-29-9

ALSO AVAILABLE FROM BLUE ANGEL®

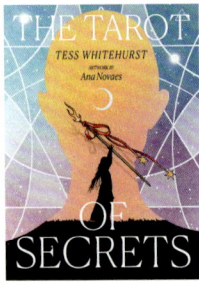

THE TAROT OF SECRETS
A formulary, catalyst, and key
Tess Whitehurst • Artwork by Ana Novaes

The Tarot of Secrets, from renowned author Tess Whitehurst, offers the formula to unlock and embody these mysteries through your own transcendent DNA. Artist Ana Novaes re-imagines Tarot for the 21st century, weaving together traditional esoteric symbolism and everyday experience to produce an evocative deck that will be loved by novices and collectors alike.

78 Cards & Guidebook Set • ISBN: 978-1-922574-45-9

ALSO AVAILABLE FROM BLUE ANGEL®

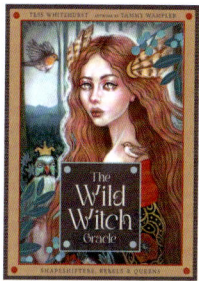

THE WILD WITCH ORACLE
Shapeshifters, Rebels & Queens
Tess Whitehurst • Artwork by Tammy Wampler

Featuring 44 bold heroines voiced by author Tess Whitehurst and beautifully illustrated by artist Tammy Wampler, *The Wild Witch Oracle* delivers messages that enliven your courage to create a life that's truly authentic. From astrological goddesses to nature sprites, faerie queens to historical monarchs, the supernatural and the human collide, awakening your innate divine powers.

44 Cards & Guidebook Set • ISBN: 978-1-922574-39-8

For more information on this
or any Blue Angel Publishing® release,
please visit our website at:

www.blueangelonline.com